James S. Hambaugh

Hambaugh's Golden Crown Receipt Book,

And Budget of Useful Information

James S. Hambaugh

Hambaugh's Golden Crown Receipt Book,
And Budget of Useful Information

ISBN/EAN: 9783337271954

Printed in Europe, USA, Canada, Australia, Japan

Cover: Foto ©Lupo / pixelio.de

More available books at **www.hansebooks.com**

HAMBAUGH'S GOLDEN CROWN

RECEIPT BOOK,

AND BUDGET OF USEFUL INFORMATION.

Aside from the large amount of useful information, this book contains a complete list of all the Leading Business Houses, Manufactories, &c., inside of

BROWN COUNTY, ILLINOIS,

To which we should direct special attention, as it will be of much benefit and interest to everybody.

THE AUTHOR AND PUBLISHER OF THIS BOOK, HAS SO ADMIRABLY AND COM-
PLETELY COMPILED AND ARRANGED ITS PAGES, AS TO MAKE IT A
MOST USEFUL AND DESIRABLE WORK; AND IN FACT IT WILL
BE FOUND AN INVALUABLE COMPANION TO EVERY
HOUSEHOLD THROUGHOUT THE WHOLE LENGTH
AND BREADTH OF OUR LAND. TAKE THIS
ONE HOME WITH YOU, READ IT
CAREFULLY, AND PRESERVE
IT FOR FUTURE USE.

PUBLISHED BY
JAMES S. HAMBAUGH,
(Editor and Publisher of the GAZETTE,)
MOUNT STERLING, ILLINOIS.

He that is of a merry heart hath a continued feast.

RECEIPTS, &C.

Peach Jam, or Marmalade.—The fruit for this preserve must be quite ripe and perfectly sound. Pare, stone, weigh, and boil it quickly for three-quarters of an hour, and do not fail to stir it often during the time ; draw it from the fire, and mix with it ten ounces of well-refined sugar, rolled or beaten to powder, for each pound of the peaches ; clear it carefully from the scum and boil it briskly for five minutes ; add the strained juice of one or two good lemons ; continue the boiling for three minutes only, and pour out the marmalade. Two minutes after the sugar is stirred to the fruit add the blanched kernels of part of the peaches.

Apple Custard Pies.—Grate, or stew to a pulp, twelve large apples ; to this add a tablesponful of salt, sugar, nutmeg, three eggs well beaten, a pint of cream or milk and a teaspoonful of melted butter, the grated rind of two lemons and the juice of one ; pour the mixture into plates lined with rich paste, and arrange strips in a network over the top ; bake a light brown, and sift over them powdered sugar.

Derby Short Cake.—Rub half a pound of butter into one pound of flour, and mix one egg, a quarter of a pound of sifted sugar, and as much milk as will make a paste. Roll this out thin, and cut the cakes with any fancy shapes or the top of a wineglass. Place on tin plates ; strew over with sugar, or cover the top of each with icing, and bake for ten minutes.

To Increase the Sharpness and Strength of Vinegar.—Boil two quarts of good vinegar till reduced to one ; then put it in a vessel, and set it in the sun for a week. Now mix the vinegar, with six times its quantity of bad vinegar, in a small cask ; it will not only mend it, but make it strong and agreeable.

Death to House Flies.—The following mixture is recommended as "sure death" to house flies : Half a spoonful of black pepper in powder, one teaspoonful of cream and a teaspoonful of sugar ; mix them well together, and place them in a room where the flies are troublesome, and they will soon disappear. It won't cost much to try it.

Removing Grease Spots out of Silk.—Take a lump of magnesia, and rub it wet over the spot ; let it dry, then brush the powder off, and the spot will disappear ; or, take a visiting card, separate it, and rub the spot with the soft internal part, and it will disappear without taking the gloss off the silk.

All pains and aches are instantly cured by the use of Hambaugh's Plantation Liniment.

THOMAS H. LYNCH,

DEALER IN

FOREIGN AND DOMESTIC .

DRY GOODS!

HATS AND CAPS,

BOOTS AND SHOES,

AND

FANCY GOODS!

☞The Best and Cheapest House in Illinois.

☞I will sell more goods for $20, than any other house will for $25.

North Side Main Street,

MOUNT STERLING, - ILLINOIS.

Stop gulping down pills, and use Hambaugh's Cathartic and Liver Syrup, which is pleasant to take, and much better in its results.

A Cure for Low Spirits.—Exercise for the body, occupation for the mind; these are the grand constituents of health and happiness, the cardinal points upon which everything turns. Motion seems to be a great preserving principle of nature, to which even inanimate things are subject; f r the winds, waves, the earth itself, are restless, and the waving of trees, shrubs, and flowers is known to be an essential part of their economy. A fixed rule of taking several hours' exercise every day, if possible, in the open air, if not, under cover, will be almost certain to secure one exemption from disease, as well as from attacks of low spirits, *ennui*—that monster who is ever waylaying the rich indolent.

"Throw but a stone, the giant dies."

Low spirits cannot exist in the atmosphere of bodily and mental activity.

To Cure Rheumatism.—This awful disease is soon alleviated, and almost invariably cured by the use of "HAMBAUGH'S CELEBRATED PLANTATION LINIMENT." The body should be kept warm by wearing a goodly quantity of woolen clothes, and the afflicted parts well saturated with the Liniment at least twice or three times a day. And as often as convenient, heat the medicine well in with a hot iron or fire shovel. This receipt will cure ninety-nine cases out of a hundred.

Corn Beer.—Take a pint of corn, boil it until soft, and add to it a gallon of water sweetened with a pint of brown sugar. Cork it tightly and set it in a warm place, and put into it a *small quantity* of yeast if the weather is cold. In warm weather omit the yeast. Add a few roots of bruised ginger, and a few sliced lemons. The same corn will answer for a year. When you pour out a pitcherful of beer, put in one of sweetened water.

Blackberry Wine.—The following is said to be an excellent receipt for the manufacture of superior wine from blackberries: Measure your berries and bruise them, to every gallon adding one quart of boiling water; let the mixture stand twenty-four hours, stirring occasionally; then strain off the liquor into a cask, to every gallon adding two pounds of sugar; cork tight, and let stand till the following October, and you will have wine ready for use, without any further straining or boiling, that will make lips smack as they never smacked, under similar influence before.

Baked Pears.—Take half a dozen fine pears; peel, cut them in halves, and take out the cores, put them into a pan with a little red wine and some cloves, half a pound of sugar and some water; set them in a moderate oven till tender, then put them on a slow fire to stew gently; add grated lemon-peel, and more sugar, if necessary; they will be sufficiently red.

Sore Throat.—The worst case of Sore Throat may be cured in one night, by using a gargle made by heating together in a cup, 1 tablespoonful of honey, 2 tablespoonfuls of vinegar, 1 tablespoonful of butter, and water enough to make half pint. Also add one red peper: steep

He that loses his conscience, hath nothing left that is worth keeping.

Never open the door to a little vice, least a great one should enter also.

awhile on the fire and use. After which rub the neck thoroughly with *Plantation Liniment*, and you are cured. In fact, the gargle is seldom if ever necessary, as the Liniment itself will cure it.

Corn Starch Pudding.—Stir three or four tablespoonfuls of starch into a pint of boiling milk, and when quite thick take it from the fire and set it aside to cool. Then mix with it half a pound of sugar, a quarter of a pound of butter, and eight eggs beaten separately and light, and beat all well together. Season with essence of lemon.

Kempton Pudding.—One pint of sour milk; half a cup of cream; one egg; one cup of blueberries; a little salt and saleratus; flour enough to make a stiff batter; steam two hours.

Frozen Peaches.—Pare and slice close. Beat rich cream (or condensed milk) with powdered sugar and white of an egg, first beaten to froth. Put peaches in freezer, pour prepared cream over. Leave as in making ice-cream. A delicious dish.

Bottle Cement for Wines and Cordials.—Take half-pound of black rosin, half-pound of red sealing-wax, and a quarter of an ounce of beeswax. Melt them all together in a pipkin, or iron pot. When it froths up before all is melted, stir it with a tallow-candle, which will settle the froth until all is melted and fit for use.

Corn Beer.—Boil a pint of corn till it is soft and add to it one pint of molasses and one gallon of water. Shake them well together in a jug and set it in a warm place. In twenty-four hours a nice beer will be produced. When this is gone add more molasses and water. The corn will answer for several weeks. A little yeast occasionally forwards fermentation.

To Cure Neuralgia.—To cure Neuralgia, all that is necessary, is to make a free use of Hambaugh's Plantation Liniment.

Strawberry Jam.—Allow equal weights of pounded loaf sugar and of strawberries; mash them in the preserving pan, and mix the sugar well with it; stir, scum, and boil it for twenty minutes.

Johnny Cake.—There are as many johnny cakes as there are cooks. Hundres of corn messes are made up, and called by their makers johnny cake, every one as like a genuine johnny cake as a mud-turtle is like a king—not much more so.

To construct a legitimate, good corn cake of this name, scald coarsely ground yellow corn-meal. Stir in an even teaspoonful of salt and two spoonfuls of any cooking fat to each pound of meal. Make the batter so stiff that it will lift heaping on a spoon. Have a dripping-pan as hot as it can be handled, and well greased. Lay in the batter an inch thick, and bake in a quick oven till the crust is a rather dark, rich brown.

How they Wash.—In the way of getting up linen and other dainty fabrics, there are none who can beat the Dutch. In their own country they use no machines—borax is the magic word. This article, refined, is liberally employed as a powder instead of soda, in the proportion of

GIVENS & CURRY,

WHOLESALE AND RETAIL

GROCERS!

MOUNT STERLING, ILL.

The above Mammoth Grocery Establishment, is constantly receiving large and new additions to their stock of

GROCERIES,
PROVISIONS,
TINWARE,
NOTIONS,
TROPICAL FRUITS,
CANDIES,
CANNED FRUITS,
ESSENCES,
CUTLERY, &c.,
and sell them at Prices to

DEFY COMPETITION!

They also pay the highest price at all times, in Cash or Goods, for all kinds of Produce, &c: Such as Corn, Oats, Vegetables, Green and Dried Fruits, Poultry, Eggs, Butter, &c., &c.

DON'T FAIL TO GIVE US A CALL!

Settle your disputes yourself, if you would make an end of them; would you prolong them, call in lawyers.

a large handful to about six gallons of boiling water—cambrics and laces requiring a somewhat stronger solution. In addition to other advantages, a saving of one half the soap is thus secured.

Dyspepsia, Indisgestion, Liver Complaint, Affections of the Kidney and Bladder, Spleen &c., are cured by Hambaugh's *Cathartic and Liver Syrup*. Try it.

Cleaning Tinware.—No acids shoulds be employed to clean tin-ware, because they attack the metal and remove it from the iron on which it forms a thin coat. We refer to articles made of tinplate, which consists of iron covered with tin. Rub the article first with rotten stone and sweet oil, then finish with whitening and a piece of soft leather. Articles made wholly of tin should be cleansed in the same manner. In a dry atmosphere planished tin-ware will remain bright for a long period, but they soon become tarnished in moist air.

Night Air.—An extraordinary fallacy is the dread of night air. What air can we breathe at night, but night air? The choice is between pure night air from without and foul air from within. Most people prefer the latter. An unaccountable choice. What will they say, if it is proved to be true that fully one-half of all the disease we suffer from is occasioned by people sleeping with their windows shut? An open window, most nights in the year, can never hurt any one. This is not to say that light is not necessary for recovery. In great cities, night air is often the best and purest air to be had in the twenty-four hours. I could better understand shutting the windows in town during the day than during the night, for the sake of the sick. The absence of smoke, the quiet, all tend to make night the best time for airing the patient.

One of our highest medical authorities on consumption and climate, has told me that the air in London is never so good as after ten o'clock at night. Always air your room then from the outside air, if possible. Windows are to open, doors are made to shut—a truth which seems extremely difficult of apprehension. Every room must be aired from without—every passage from within. But the fewer passages there are in a hospital, the better.

How to Prevent a Cow from Kicking while Milking.—Take a linen cloth, wet it in cold water, and just before you commence milking, lay it on their loins wet. Those who have tried it say that a cow will not kick so long as the cold wet cloth remains on her back

A Cooling Drink.—As nearly every person is inquiring for some cooling drink during this hot weather, we give the following recipe for a refreshing and invigorating beverage, which has been recommended by an eminent physician. It is an effervescing drink, but far better than soda-water, as the effervescene is much more slow: Two ounces of tartaric acid, two pounds of white sugar, the juice of half a lemon, and three pints of water. Boil them together five minutes, and when nearly cold add the whites of three eggs, well beaten, with half a cup of flour, and half an ounce of wintergreen or other flavoring. Bottle and keep

The way to gain a good reputation is to endeavor to be what you desire to appear.

THOS H. CASTEEN. JOSEPHUS CASTEEN.

CASTEEN BROS.,

DEALERS IN

DRY GOODS!

Clothing, Hats and Caps, Boots and Shoes, Shawls, Hardware, Queensware, Glassware, Cutlery, Powder and Shot,

GROCERIES AND PROVISIONS!

&c., &c., &c,

We will NOT BE UNDERSOLD!

Don't fail to give us a trial before buying elsewhere.

BAKERY!

F. MILLER, Proprietor.

FRESH BREAD, CAKES, PIES, OYSTERS,

CANNED FRUITS, &c., always on hand.

DON'T FAIL TO GIVE US A CALL!

North Side Main Street, MT. STERLING, ILL.

E. MEYER,

MERCHANT TAILOR

AND DEALER IN

CLOTH, BEAVER, CHINCHILLA,

Crape of all colors, Ready-made Clothing, Hats and Caps, Gloves and a general assortment of Gents' Furnishing Goods always on hand, and will sell as cheap as the cheapest for CASH Remember that I will not be undersold. Cutting of Men's and Boys' Garments promptly and neatly executed. Will be found on South Side of Main Street,

MOUNT STERLING, ILLINOIS.

2

Burns, Stings and Bites of Insects are instantly cured by the use of Hambaugh's Plantation Liniment.

It in a cold place. Take two tablespoonful of this syrhp for a tumbler of water, and add one quarter of a teaspoonful of soda, stir it and then drink.

Hambaugh's Cathartic and Liver Syrup Cleanses the system, purifies the blood and sets the machinery of the human body in good repair, and starts it to going. And all that is necessary to keep it in motion, and in a healthy condition, is to occasionally resort to this Syrup. The afflicted should all try it and test its magic virtues.

Broiled Mutton Cutlets.—Take the best end of a neck of mutton, which will give seven chops, saw four inches off the end of the upper rib bone ; the piece thus trimmed off is used for broiled breast of mutton. Saw off the chine bone, and cut the seven chops, clearing the meat an inch off the end of each bone. Flatten them with a bat, and remove the gristle from round the lean, and pare away the meat and skin from the inside of each bone; this is to give the cutlets the required shape. Sprinkle the cutlets on each side with two pinches of salt and one of pepper, oil them slightly and put them on a gridiron over a brisk fire; cook them four minutes on one side and three on the other; dish up in a circle and serve."

A Good Way to Keep Hams.—Wrap them in good, sweet hay, then inclose them in a tight bag, and hang in the granary. The nicest cold ham I ever saw was over a year old, and had been kept in the manner described.

New Potatoes, a la Francaise.—Skin, wash, and wipe dry some early potatoes ; melt some butter in a stewpan ; when it is quite hot place the potatoes in it, simmer them slowly, turn them occasionally, and when done take them up and place them in another stewpan, with sufficient fresh butter to form a sauce, shake them over the fire merely till the butter is melted, arrange them in a dish, pour the butter over them and strew a little fine salt upon them, serve as hot as possible. In Italy olive oil is employed instead of butter, and is really preferable.

Cauliflower Omelette.—Take the white part of a boiled cauliflower after it is cold, and chop it very small, and mix with it a sufficient quantity of well-beaten egg, to make a very thick batter, then fry it in fresh butter, in a small pan, and send it to the table hot.

Cholera Morbus.—This is a disease common to warm climates, and is characterized by vomiting, purging, coldness and cramps of the extremities, and violent griping. The following is a good receipt for its cure. One tablespoonful of ground black pepper, one-half tablespoonful salt, warm water one-half tumblerful, one-third tumblerful of cider vinegar. Dose a tablespoonful every 15 to 20 minutes, until all is taken, or the disease checked. Stir and mix well before taking each time.

Ocean Cake.—To one cup of milk add two cups of sugar ; one half cup of butter ; the whites of five eggs, well beaten ; three cups of flour ; two teaspoonsful of cream of tartar, and one of soda. Flavor to your taste.

Labor lost—an organ-grinder playing at the door of a deaf and dumb asylum.

Philosophical happiness is to want little and enjoy much; vulgar happiness is to want much and enjoy little.

Ice Cream.—We give the following as an excellent recipe for making ice cream: Fresh cream one-half gallon; rich milk one-half gallon; white sugar one pound. Dissolve the sugar in the mixture, flavor with extract to suit your taste, or take the peel from a fresh lemon and steep one-half of it in as little water as you can, and add this—it makes the lemon flavor better than the extract—and no flavor will so universally please as the lemon; keep the same proportion for any amount desired. The juice of strawberries or raspberries gives a beautiful color and flavor to ice creams; or about one-half ounce of essence or extracts to a gallon. Have your ice well broken; one quart of salt to a pail of ice. About half an hour's constant stirring and occasional scraping down and beating together, will freeze it. The old fashioned freezer will make very smooth and nice ice cream.

Home Cheerfulness.—Many a child goes astray, not because there is a want of prayer or virtue at home, but simply because home lacks sunshine. A child needs smiles as much as flowers need sunbeams. Children look little beyond the present moment. If a thing pleases they are apt to seek it; if it displeases they are prone to avoid it. If home is the place where faces are sour, and words harsh, and fault-finding is ever in the ascendant, they will spend as many hours as possible elsewhere. Let every father and mother, then, try to be happy. Let them talk to their children, especially the little ones, in such a way as to make them happy.

Winter Rules.—Never go to bed with cold or damp feet. In going into a colder air, keep the mouth resolutely closed, that by compelling the air to pass circuitously through the nose and head, it may become warmed before it reaches the lungs, and thus prevent those shocks and sudden chills, which frequently end in pleurisy, pneumonia, and other serious forms of disease. Never sleep with the head in the draught of an open door or window. Let more covering be on the lower limbs than on the body. Have an extra covering within easy reach in case of a sudden and great change of weather during the night. Never stand still a moment out of doors, especially at street corners, after having walked even a short distance. Never ride near the open window of a vehicle for a single half-minute, especially if it has been preceded by a walk; valuable lives have thus been lost, or good health permanently destroyed. Never put on a new boot or shoe in the beginning of a walk.

Erysipelas, Chronic Eruptions, Chilblains, Corns, Tetter and Ringworms are all easily cured by using HAMBAUGH'S PLANTATION LINIMENT, *the Lion of Medicines.*

For the Sick—Restorative Jelly.—Take a leg of well-fed pork, just as cut up, beat it, and break the bone. Set it over a gentle fire, with three gallons of water, and simmer to one. Let half an ounce of mace, and the same of nutmegs, stew in it. Strain through a fine sieve. When cold, take off the fat. Give a chocolate cup the first and last thing, and at noon, adding salt to suit the taste. This is very valuable in all cases of debility where animal food is admissible.

A bad custom must not plead its age as reason for longer life and larger growth.

Hambaugh's Plantation Liniment is the Lion of Medicines.

Vegetable Soup.—Take one potato, one turnip, and one onion, with a little colery or colery seed. Slice and boil for half an hour in one quart of water. Salt to the taste, and pour the whole upon a piece of dry toast. This forms a good substitute for animal food, and may be used when the latter would be improper.

Lying in Bed.—It is often a question among people who are unacquainted with the anatomy and physiology of men, whether lying with head exalted or on a level with the body is the most unwholesome. Most, consulting their own case on this point, argue in favor of that which they prefer. Now, although many delight in bolstering up their heads at night, and sleep soundly without injury, yet we declare it to be a dangerous habit. The vessels in which the blood passes from the heart to the head are always lessened in their cavities when the head is resting in bed higher than the body; therefore, in all diseases attended with fever, the head should be pretty nearly on a level with the body; and people ought to accustom themselves to sleep thus, and avoid danger.

Hambaugh's Champion Grease Exterminator is considered the very best now in use. It extracts grease, paint and spots, from the finest silk or linen, without coloring it in the least. No lady or gentleman should be without it. And in fact every family should keep it in the house. For sale by all Druggists and Grocers.

Gum Acacia Restorative.—Take two ounces of pure white gum Arabic, procure the lump, the powdered is very apt to be adulterated—pulverize it well, and dissolve by the aid of a gentle heat in a gill of water, stirring constantly. When it is entirely dissolved, add three tablespoonfuls of pure strained honey. Let it remain over the fire until it becomes of the consistence of a jelly. The heat must be very gentle; it must not boil. If desirable, flavor with lemon or vanilla. This will be found a very pleasant article of diet for delicate stomachs. When the articles used are pure, it will be transparent and of a light golden color. This will be borne by the weakest stomach, when every thing else is rejected. It is *highly nutritious.*

Sponge Cake.—No better recipe for ordinary use can be obtained than the following: one cup of sugar, one cup of sweet milk, one egg, two teaspoonfuls of cream of tartar, one third cup of butter, and two cups of flour. Flavor with one half teaspoonful of the essence of lemon.

Lemon Extract.—Both lemon and orange rinds make good extracts—allow two ounces of strongly flavored rinds to half a pint of alcohol; adding a few drops of the oil will greatly improve the extract.

Corn Pudding.—Can't any one make "mush?" Yes, very likely, after a fashion; at least we should think a great many of the meal messes we have tasted were manufactured by parties not overstocked with wisdom in that direction—lumpy, salvy, slushy, scorched stuff, tasting like raw corn slightly smoked. That is not pudding such as Christians ought to eat. To make it good, the meal should first be mixed with warm water into a thin batter, and vigorously stirred until no

Passion is the drunkenness of the mind, and therefore, in its present working, not always controllable by season.

symptom of a lump remains. Having the water in your kettle boiling moderately, pour in the batter gradually, stirring vigorously all the while, and continue the stirring for a quarter of an hour; then set the kettle back, and cook slowly another hour. Then you will have good pudding.

The Lion of Medicines.—Hambaugh's Celebrated Plantation Liniment, is justly and properly termed the "Lion of Medicines." Its wide spead reputation is fast sweeping over our continent, and it is becoming a household word throughout our whole land. Disease and corruption flee before it and writhe within its grasp, as do the victims of the ferocious Lion of the African forest. Mr. Hambaugh warrants every bottle to give entire satisfaction, or he will return the money.

Dressing for Slaw.—Boil half a pint of cider vinegar with a lump of nice fresh butter, the size of an egg; cut in four bits, and roll it in flour. When boiled, pour into it the beaten yolks of three eggs, and pour hot over finely chopped cabbage; add salt and peper.

Ginger Cookies.—One cup molasses; one cup sugar; one cup butter; one half cup lard; one half cup butter milk; one and a half large teaspoonfuls soda; one egg; one tablespoonful ginger; knead soft, cut in squares, and bake in a quick oven. Excellent. Try it.

Apple Custard Pie—The Nicest Pie ever Eaten.—This recipe is hardly in season, but our readers can keep it for reference when needed. Peel sour apples and stew until soft and not much water left in them; then rub them through a cullender; beat three eggs for each pie to be baked, and put in at the rate of one cup of butter and one of sugar for three pies; season with nutmeg. One egg for each pie will do very well, but the amount of sugar must be governed somewhat by the acidity of the apples. Bake as pumpkin pies, which they resemble in appearance. Dried apples are very nice by making them a little more juicy. You can frost them, and return them to the oven for a few moments, which will improve their appearance.

Headache.—Headache is almost instantaenously cured by the use of Hambaugh's Plantation Liniment. Try it.

Foul Cisterns.—The annoyance of foul smelling cistern-water is known to most people. No "cleaning out" of the cistern seems to avail long against it. It comes from decaying vegetable or animal matter from the roof, and a simple and inexpensive remedy is found in the application of an ounce of permanganate of potassa for every fifteen gallons of water, which insures the chemical destruction of the offensive elements.

Corn Meal Pudding in Paste.—Beat the yolks of six eggs well; add to them three-quarters of a pound of butter which has been creamed, the rind of one lemon and juice of two, sugar and nutmeg to your taste, and two pounds of mush moderately warm. Bake in paste as lemon pudding. It is very nice with preserves on the paste.

Variegated Pound Cake.—Beat to a cream three-fourths of a pound

If it is only "conscience that makes cowards of us all," most men should be fearless as Cæsar.

3

of butter and one pound of white sugar. Mix in with them the well-beaten whites of sixteen eggs, and stir in gradually one pound of sifted flour. Flavor with rose-water or lemon. Pulverize one drachm of cochineal, the same quantity of alum, a drachm of soda and one of cream of tartar; pour over them two tablespoonfuls of boiling water, and strain through a piece of thin muslin. Incorporate this thoroughly with one-eighth of the batter. Pour into a buttered mould a layer of white batter, and then a *thin* layer of the rose-colored batter, and proceed thus until all the batter is in. Finally pass a knife-blade four or five times through the batter to variegate it finely. This quantity of coloring is sufficient for two pounds of cake.

Currant and Almond Cake.—A pound and a half of sugar, the same of flour, a pound of butter, six eggs. Mix, and beat well, as pound-cake, and add a pound and a half of currants, and half a pound of blanched almonds cut in thin slices and put in last.

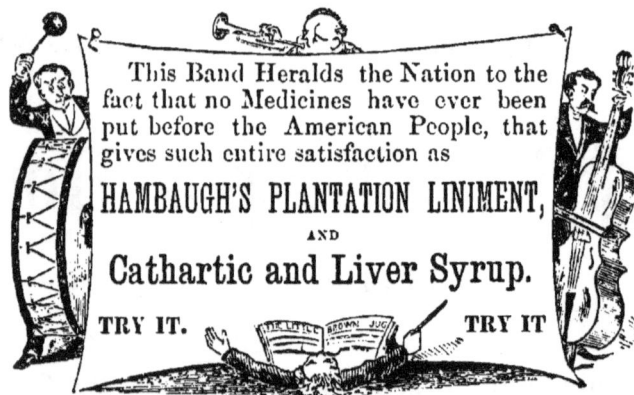
Wild Ducks.—After they are cleaned and ready for cooking, wrap them in a clean cloth, and bury twelve hours in the earth, to remove the strong flavor of this bird. They are usually cooked without stuffing. Three-quarters of an hour will be sufficient to cook them. When you dish it, draw a sharp knife three times through the breast, and pour over a gravy of a little hot butter, the juice of a lemon, a sprinkling of cayenne pepper, and a wineglass of port wine. This is poured over as they go on the table.

Hashed Clams.—Chop clams fine; stew them in very little water, add

Dangerous navigation is doubly dangerous in doubling the "cape" of a pretty coquette.

their own juice; boil fifteen minutes, and season with butter and pepper; after taking up the hash, thicken the gravy with a yolk or two of eggs.

Montgomery Pudding.—Take thin slices of sponge cake, and put into a deep dish until it is half full. Grate over the cake the rind of a lemon, squeeze the juice into the dish, and put in wine or brandy enough to moisten the cake well. Then make a custard with milk, eggs and sugar, and fill the dish, and set into a moderate oven and bake a light brown. When it is done and cold, make an icing of whites of eggs and sugar, as for cake, and spread over the top of the pudding thickly, and brown it in the oven. Serve cold.

Gelatine Jelly without Boiling or Straining.—To a package of gelatine take a pint of cold water, the juice of three lemons, and the rind of one. Let it stand an hour, and then add three pints of boiling water, a pint of wine, and two pounds and a quarter of white crushed sugar. A wineglassful of brandy will improve the flavor. Pour into moulds, and set in a cool place.

Red Currant Pudding, Baked.—Red currant pudding may be made in the usual way, with a pudding crust and boiled; or it can be made by pressing the fruit through a sieve, so as to free it from the pipes, which are very disagreeable; then, to a pint of pulp add two ounces of breadcrumbs and a quarter of a pound of sugar; put it into a tart-dish with a rim of puff-paste; serve with cream or custard. White currants may be treated in the same manner.

Orange Cream.—Dissolve one ounce of isinglass and six ounces of loaf-sugar in a pint of boiling milk, having first rubbed off the rind of five oranges with some of the lumps of sugar. Extract the juice of the oranges, and then strain the isinglass and other ingredients into it; add one gill of cream, and the yolks of four eggs, which must be well beaten. Pour the whole into a saucepan, warm it over the fire, but do not allow it to boil; pour into a basin and stir it until cold, before you put it into a mould.

A receipt for coloring brown from materials which can be procured in the woods. It will color any shade from a light cinnamon to a very dark brown, according to the strength of the dye: Take the bark of the common alder, boil it an hour; having sufficient water to cover the goods; add a very little copperas; dip in the articles to be colored; let them remain about ten minutes; wring them out, and then dip them into a very weak lye—previously prepared—wring them out immediately, and wash them in soap and soft water.

Sponge Pudding.—Three eggs, the weight of the eggs in sugar, butter, and flour. One teaspoonful of cream tartar, and half teaspoonful of soda dissolved in a little lemon. To be eaten with wine sauce.

A chap says he cured palpitation of the heart by the application of another palpitating heart to the part affected.

Disease and corruption flee with terror before the healing grasp of the Lion of Medicine.

Sponge Pudding.—One quart of milk, one cup of flour, salt, seven eggs bake one hour or more, and eat with sauce ; rich cream sauce is very nice.

Superior Cake.—One egg, one cup sugar, one-half cup butter, one cup sweet milk, one teaspoonful soda, and two teaspoonsfuls cream tartar. Flavor with lemon or vanilla.

Ostrich Feathers.—Dissolve some fine white soap in boiling soft water, and add a piece of pearl-ash. When the water is just cool enough for the hand to bear it, pass the feathers through it several times, squeezing them gently with the hand. Repeat the same process with a weaker solution of soap, and then rinse the feathers in cold water, beating them across the hand to get rid of the water. When they are nearly dry, draw each fibre over the edge of a small blunt knife, turning it round in the direction you wish the curl to take. If the feather is to be flat, place it between the leaves of a book, to press it.

The Young, the Old, the Middle Aged are all made happy by the use of
HAMBAUGH'S MEDICINES!
TRY THEM.

Those who can not take pills, should use Hambaugh's Cathartic and Liver Syrup. It is pleasant to take, besides it is much more efficacious in its effects than Pills. It operates directly on the billiary derangements of the system, and thoroughly cleanses the whole body from all billious disorders. Besides it does not contain any mercury whatever, but is purely vegetable. We hope that the afflicted who may read this notice will purchase a bottle of this great medicine the first opportunity, and if it proves otherwise than what we say, their money will be cheerfully refunded. Try it.

Remedy Against Moths.—An ounce of gum camphor, and one of powdered shell of red pepper, are macerated in eight ounces of strong alcohol for seven days, then strained. With this tincture the furs or clothes are sprinkled over and rolled up in sheets. This remedy is used in Russia under the name of the Chinese tincture for moths.

Dyeing White Gloves a Beautiful Purple.—Boil four ounces of log-

The christian is very frequently only Bible the world will ever read. How sad that the copy should be so defaced.

E. F. CRANE & SON,

ARE CONSTANTLY RECEIVING

DRY GOODS!

OF EVERY DESCRIPTION.

READY-MADE CLOTHING,

FOR BOY'S AND MEN.

BOOTS & SHOES,

Of the best Makes and Warranted Work.

HATS AND CAPS,

SCHOOL BOOKS,

WALL PAPER,

CARPETS AND OIL CLOTHS,

Groceries and Queensware!

All of which have been bought cheap, and will be sold for a small profit.

WOOL!

Bought for Cash or exchanged for Manufactured Goods.

MOUNT STERLING, ILL.

Most of the shadows that cross our path through life are caused by our standing in our own light.

wood and two ounces of roche-alum, in three pints of soft water, till half wasted. Let it stand to be cold after straining. Let the gloves be nicely mended; then do them over with a brush, and when dry repeat it. Twice is sufficient, unless the color is to be very dark. When dry, rub off the loose dye with a course cloth. Beat up the white of an egg, and with a sponge rub it over the leather. The dye will stain the hands, but wetting them with vinegar before washing, will take it off.

Black Reviver, for Faded Mourning Dresses, Black Coats, &c.—1. Boil in two pints of water down to one, two ounces of Aleppo galls, in powder, two ounces of logwood, one of gum Arabic; then add one ounce of sulphate of iron. This may be evaporated to a powder. 2. Galls, eight ounces; logwood, green vitrol, iron filings, sumach, of each one ounce; vinegar, two pints.

Whitewash that will not rub off.—Slake the lime in the usual way. Mix one gill of flour with a little cold water, taking care to beat out all the lumps; then pour on boiling water enough to thicken it to the consistency of common starch when boiled for use. Pour it while hot into a bucket of the slaked lime, and add one pound of whitening. Stir all well together. A little "blue water" made by squeezing the indigo bag, or a little pulverised indigo mixed with water, improves it.

Hambaugh's Plantation Liniment, alleviates more pains and aches, than any other medicine manufactured in the world. Try it! Try it!!

Mulled Wine.—Take a bottle of Madeira or sherry wine, a pint and a half of water, and put it to boil in a tea-kettle; while the wine is boiling, beat up the yolks of twelve eggs; add one pound of fine white sugar, and a grated nutmeg; stir it all together; beat the whites to a froth, and beat it into the yolks; when the wine is boiled, hold the tea-kettle as high as possible, and turn the wine on, stirring the eggs constantly; then turn it from one pitcher to another until it is all mixed.

To Protect Horses' Hoofs.—Gutta percha may be used to protect the feet of horses from tenderness and slipping. It is first cut into small pieces, and softened with hot water, then mixed with half its weight of powdered sal ammoniac, and the mixture melted in a tinned saucepan over a gentle fire, keeping it well stirred. When required for use, melt in a glue pot, scrape the hoof clean, and apply the mixture with a knife.

Excellent Bread.—Mix seven pounds of best flour with three pounds of pared boiled potatoes. Steam off the water and leave them a few minutes on the fire, mash them fine, and mix them whilst quite warm in the flour with a spoonful or more of salt. Put a quart of water, milk warm, with three large spoonfuls of yeast, gradually to the potates and flour. Work it well into a smooth dough, and let it remain four hours before it is baked.

How to Keep Butter Sweet for Years.—The butter must be well churned and worked, and packed hard and tight in kegs of seasoned white oak; the head is then put in, leaving a small hole, in which brine is

Music, says Auerbach, washes away from the soul the dust of every day life.

Plantation Liniment.

Plantation Liniment cures aches and pain,
It makes the sick all well again;
It will make young men out of old,
And is worth to you its weight in gold.

Try It!

If you are troubled with an aching head,
And almost wish that you are dead,
Take Plantation Liniment and apply thereto,
And see how quick it will bring you through.

Try It!

'Tis the "LION OF MEDICINES" we have for sale.
To effect a cure it will never fail:
Now any and all who have Rheumatic Pain,
Try Plantation Liniment and be well again.

Try It!

For Neuralgia it cannot be excelled,
It cures Toothache and Earache equally well;
It will cure a Lame Back, and in fact anywhere,
That the Plantation Liniment can be brought to bear.

Try It!

Plantation Liniment! how welcome the sound!
To mothers who have children romping around;
Who are sure to get into some kind of scrape,
That only the Liniment can bring into shape.

Try It!

Now all who may have a Pain or an Ache,
A bottle of Plantation Liniment take;
We'll warrant it to cure every thing we say—
Our motto stands forth, "No CURE, No PAY!"

Try It!

Sold by all Druggists.

4

Neuralgia can be cured by the use of Hambaugh's Plantation Liniment.

poured to fill the vacant space; and of so much importance is it deemed to prevent any bad taste, that the plug for the hole must not be made of cedar or pine, but of cypress or bass wood; as otherwise it would be injured. After which, these kegs are placed in hogsheads well filled with brine of full solution, that will bear an egg, which is then headed up tight and close. By adopting this process, butter may be made to keep in any climate.

Beautiful Experiment.—Fill a wide-mouthed glass jar with water, and cover it over with a piece of "foundation" (the ladies will understand this); cover that over with a layer of peas, pressing it down so that the peas will lie in the water. They will then swell and sprout, the roots growing down into the water, their fine fibres presenting a beautiful appearance. Set this in a window and vines will grow up which can be conducted to the sill. The whole is very handsome.

Good to Remember.—Our readers will do well to remember that Mr. Hambaugh does not weary the public mind by putting before them a long list of testimonials in regard to his Medicines. There has been, and still is being so much fraud practiced in that direction, by quacks and humbugs, that Mr. H. deems it beyond his sphere to follow in their footsteps, and aspires to a more honorable and noble way of making customers: which is by guaranteeing satisfaction in every instance; and by refunding of the money where parties are dissatisfied. Many thousands of bottles of his preparation have been sold already on these terms, and not the first instance has yet occured where he had to refund the money.

Hooping Cough.—Take powdered cantharides, powdered camphor, of each one scruple; extract of bark, three drachms. Rub these well together, and divide into powders of eight grains each. Dose—one every three or four hours. To be used only in advanced stages of the disease.

Short Crust for Sweet Pastry.—Work very lightly half a pound of butter into one pound of flour, breaking it quite small; add a little salt,

Always refuse the advice which passion gives

Dispepsia is easily cured by the use of Hambaugh's Cathartic and Liver Syrup. Try it!

two ounces of finely pulverized sugar, and sufficient milk to make it into a perfectly smooth paste. Bake it slowly and keep it pale.

To Remove Tartar from the Teeth.--1. Use the tooth-brush night and morning.   2. Once every day rub the brush lightly two or three times over a piece of soap; then dip it in salt, and with it well clean the teeth.   3. Eat freely of cress (the same as used with mustard), and with salt only. If used for two or three consecutive days it will effectually lossen the tartar of long standing. 4. The same effect is produced by eating strawberries or raspberries.

For a Cough.—Roast a large lemon very carefully, without burning it ; when it is thoroughly hot, cut and squeeze it into a cup, upon three ounces of sugar, finely powdered. Take a spoonful whenever your cough troubles you. It is as good as it is agreeable to the taste. Rarely has it been known to fail of giving relief.

Don't fail to try Hambaugh's Champion Grease Exterminator and Cleanser.

To Cure Hams.—Take half a pound of bay salt, a quarter of a pound of saltpetre, half a pound of common salt, two pounds of foot sugar, half a pound of cake salt-prunella—mixed well together ; rub the hams well, and keep them in pickle a month.

Bitters.—Take half an ounce of the yolk of fresh eggs, carefully separated from the white; half an ounce of gentian root ; one and half drachms of Seville orange peel; and one pint of boiling water.   Pour the water hot upon the above ingredients, and let them steep in it for two hours; then strain, and bottle for use.

Mulled Ale.—Boil one quart of good ale with some nutmeg, beat up six eggs, and mix them with a little cold ale, then pour the hot ale to it, and return it several times to prevent it curdling; warm, and stir it till sufficiently thick ; add a piece of butter, or a glass of brandy, and serve it with dry toast.

Mustiness in Wine.—This is easiest removed by violently agitating the wine for some time with a little of the sweetest olive or almond oil.   A little coarsly powdered fresh burnt charcoal, or even some slices of bread, toasted black, will frequently have a good effect.

To Clean and Polish Looking Glasses.—Looking Glasses and glass over pictures, can be cleaned with Hambaugh's Grease Exterminator and Cleanser, better than by any other known process. Saturate a piece of sponge or cloth with the Cleanser and after rubbing the glass thoroughly, dry it off with soft paper.

Hambaugh's Cathartic and Liver Syrup will cure disease of the Spine.

A Good Plum Cake.—An equal weight of butter and flour, a quarter of a pound of cut peels and citrons, double the weight of butter in currants, the grating of three lemons, and half a nutmeg, half an ounce of pudding spice, one glass of brandy, and the same quantity of eggs as the weight in butter ; beat your butter as for pound cake ; put in a

The vessel no woman objects to embark on—a court ship.

It is unwise to worry about what can not be helped, and foolish to worry about what can be helped. Therefore worry not at all.

---

few chopped sweet almonds. Paper and butter a hoop, bottom and sides; then put in your mixtures; bake in a slow oven for some time; take off the hoop when done, but not the paper.

Worm Lozenges.—Ginger, two ounces, jalap, one drachm; calomel, one scruple; white sugar, one once; beat well to a mass with simple syrup, and divide into twenty lozenges or cakes. Each lozenge will contain one grain of calomel. Dose—from two to four early in the morning, fasting.

Simple Cholera Preventive.—An eminent physician says the surest preventive of the Asiatic cholera is sulphur; put half a teaspoonful of flour-of-sulphur into each of your stockings and go about your business; never go out with an empty stomach; eat no fresh bread nor sour food. This is not only a preventive in cholera, but also in many other epidemic diseases.

To Clean Marble.—Take two parts of common soda, one part of pumice-stone, and one part of finely powdered chalk; sift it through a fine sieve, and mix it with water; then rub it well all over the marble, and the stains will be removed; then wash the marble over with soap and water, and it will be as clean as it was at first.

Items Worth Committing to Memory.—A bit of glue dissolved in skim milk and water will restore old crape. Half a cranberry bound on a corn will soon kill it. An inkstand was turned over upon a white table cloth, a servant threw over it a mixture of salt and pepper plentifully, and all traces of it disappeared. Picture frames and glasses are preserved from flies by painting them with a brush dipped into a mixture made by boiling three or four onions in a pint of water.

To cure Croup in children, rub the neck and breast thoroughly with Hambaugh's Plantation Liniment, after which, wrap wooled cloths around it.

Onions.—Boil in water until nearly done, and then pour over fresh hot water with milk in it. Drain, and pour over melted butter.

For Headache, use Plantation Liniment.

FRED. D. CRANE,

DEALER IN

Dry Goods,

BOOTS AND SHOES,

HATS AND CAPS,

AND

CLOTHING!

I keep the largest and most attractive stock of Goods in the City, and aim to make the price on each article so low, as to make it to the *advantage* of *every one* to buy their goods of me.

I also keep a large Stock of

FURNITURE!

up-stairs, which it will be to the interest of every one to examine before buying.

F. D. CRANE, Mount Sterling, Ill.

Good company and good conversation are the very sinews of virtue.

S. D. COX.   W. H. BRACKENRIDGE.

COX & BRACKENRIDGE,
DEALERS IN
FOREIGN & DOMESTIC DRY GOODS,
NOTIONS, CLOTHING,
HATS, CAPS, BOOTS AND SHOES,
Queensware, Hardware, Drugs,
CUTLERY, GROCERIES AND PROVISIONS,
A FULL STOCK ALWAYS ON HAND.
COOPERSTOWN, ILL.

A. D. RAVENSCROFT,
DEALER IN
DRY GOODS!
NOTIONS, CLOTHING,
Hats, Caps, Boots and Shoes,
DRUGS AND MEDICINES, TOILET ARTICLES,
Hardware, Queensware, Groceries, Provisions, Flour, Meal, Salt, &c., &c.

VERSAILLES, ILL.

A fashionable party is now called a Daughtercultural show.

HAMBAUGH'S
CELEBRATED

PLANTATION LINIMENT

JAMES S. HAMBAUGH,
PROPRIETOR,
MOUNT STERLING, ILLS.

THIS GREAT MEDICINE IS JUSTLY TITLED

THE LION OF MEDICINES

From the fact that it contains the quintessence of all other preparations as a pain killer, disease eradicator, &c., and is truly one of the most wonderful medical discoveries of the age; being the most perfect and effectual remedy ever before offered to the public, for all diseases to which a liniment is applicable. Its action upon the organization is indeed wonderful. Its volatile, penetrating, soothing and healing properties diffuse themselves to the very bone. It enters the pores of the system, and penetrates immediately to the seat of the disease, and gives a new impulse to the whole nervous system, stimulates the absorbents and secretions, and thus assists nature to throw off and rid herself of any diseased action of nerves, muscles, or ligaments, making it equally applicable to sores of any kind, rheumatism, &c., and from a diseased action of any of the structural portions of the system whatever. Possessing these peculiar powers, is the reason why it is efficacious in so many different cases.

The proprietor, in bringing this Liniment before the public, asks only a fair and unprejudiced trial of the same, feeling confident from the unprecedented reputation which it has already attained through the different parts of the country wherein it has been introduced, that those who use it will be much benefitted and doubly satisfied therewith.

This medicine is equally beneficial in all diseases of horses and other animals, and is warranted to GIVE ENTIRE SATISFACTION in every instance, or money refunded.

Let all who have not used this wonderful medicine, give it a trial, and test the magic influence of its virtues.

No family should be without it.

Try It!   *Try It!!*   *Try It!!!*

FOR SALE BY ALL DRUGGISTS.

WHOLESALE AGENTS.

Burnhams & Van Schaack, Chicago; Meyer Bros. & Co., St. Louis; F. E. Suire & Co., Cincinnati; J. B. Brown & Co., Springfield; Montgomery & Co., Quincy.

5

I will train the young to ignorance, dissipation, infidelity, and lewd ness.—*Rumseller.*

www.ingramcontent.com/pod-product-compliance
Lightning Source LLC
Chambersburg PA
CBHW021452090426
42739CB00009B/1730